A Personal Leadership Philosophy

Written by
Paul D. Cummings

~ A Personal Leadership Philosophy ~

A Personal Leadership Philosophy

Another Fine Offering From

~ The Fire Press ~

ISBN 0-9655098-2-6

Published by **Level 10 Publications**
1860 Pope Creek Road
Wildwood, Georgia 30757
1-800-823-7698 • 706-820-9728

Introduction

Great Leaders have the ability to create a vision that burns so bright that the vision eradicates all doubt. They have the ability to make their vision clear, concise, compelling, engaging and, most of all, consistent. This special brand of leadership consistency comes about when a leader develops a personal leadership philosophy.

That is a philosophy that supports -- in every way -- the leader's vision for life and business. My purpose in writing this book was to provide any individual who aspires to be a great leader with a road map to greatness. The first key to greatness is to begin to develop your own *Personal Leadership Philosophy* that clearly defines who you are, what you stand for, and most importantly, what you believe in. By taking this magical step, you will begin to clarify who you are as a leader to everyone around you.

A personal leadership philosophy serves as an internal compass that clearly defines personal and corporate conduct on a daily basis. Remember, you can't get lost on a straight track. By adopting the principles in this book, you can lay a track from where you are to your biggest corporate and personal dreams. Begin today to build your personal leadership philosophy. As your new journey begins, always look for ways to expand, magnify and modify, when necessary, your personal leadership philosophy. Share your new-found leadership philosophy with all the important people in your life so they can fully understand who you are and what you stand for on a daily basis.

If you enjoy this book, please contact Paul D. Cummings World Wide Enterprises and order my new book, *Lessons At The Fence Post - Volume II*.

- Paul D. Cummings

Dedicated to
George and Shirley Cummings

Thanks for being the greatest
parents on earth.

I will focus on continual education every day.

–Paul D. Cummings

I will pass positives down and negatives up every day.

–Paul D. Cummings

I will be a fountain of enthusiasm every day.

–Paul D. Cummings

I will operate with unbridled energy every day.

–Paul D. Cummings

I will be a prisoner of nothing every day.

–Paul D. Cummings

I will guard my integrity like a sacred thing every day.

–Paul D. Cummings

I will greet every person I meet with love in my heart every day.

–Paul D. Cummings

I will be goal-directed every day.

–Paul D. Cummings

I will uphold the standards of our organization every day.

–Paul D. Cummings

I will pursue perfection and tolerate nothing less than excellence every day.

–Paul D. Cummings

I will operate with the utmost integrity in all my actions every day.

–Paul D. Cummings

I will create a clear vision for others to follow every day.

–Paul D. Cummings

I will focus like a laser beam on success every day.

–Paul D. Cummings

I will be passionate about our corporate mission every day.

–Paul D. Cummings

I will require our people to read new books to expand their knowledge every day.

–Paul D. Cummings

I will be determined in my efforts every day.

–Paul D. Cummings

I will require our people to prospect for new business every day.

–Paul D. Cummings

I will continue to develop a personal learning library every day.

–Paul D. Cummings

I will play like I am in first place and practice like I am in last place every day.

–Paul D. Cummings

I will be true to my personal values every day.

–Paul D. Cummings

I will demand that our team members deliver premium care to our valued customers every day.

–Paul D. Cummings

I will have a positive winning attitude every day.

–Paul D. Cummings

I will utilize new technology to improve our organization every day.

–Paul D. Cummings

I will be open to the ideas of others every day.

–Paul D. Cummings

I will display interest in our team members' personal goals and dreams every day.

–Paul D. Cummings

I will love to win and hate to lose every day.

–Paul D. Cummings

I will be a teacher for all those people I lead every day.

–Paul D. Cummings

I will coach those players who need to be coached every day.

–Paul D. Cummings

I will ask our people to treat others the way they would like to be treated every day.

–Paul D. Cummings

I will respect, but not fear our competition every day.

–Paul D. Cummings

I will focus on the activities we must complete to win every day.

–Paul D. Cummings

I will hold our team members instantaneously accountable every day.

–Paul D. Cummings

I will bring the fire into the battle every day.

–Paul D. Cummings

I will operate with compassion every day.

–Paul D. Cummings

I will be a consistent leader every day.

–Paul D. Cummings

I will be a likeable person for those around me every day.

–Paul D. Cummings

I will require our people to write handwritten thank you notes to our customers every day.

–Paul D. Cummings

I will be a crusader for doing what is right every day.

–Paul D. Cummings

I will operate with a pure spirit of intent every day.

–Paul D. Cummings

I will check my ego at the door every day.

–Paul D. Cummings

I will operate with a high level of self-confidence in all my actions every day.

–Paul D. Cummings

I will catch our people doing something right every day.

–Paul D. Cummings

I will do something nice for someone and not get caught every day.

–Paul D. Cummings

I will require our leaders to actively coach their players every day.

–Paul D. Cummings

I will stay away from negative influences every day.

–Paul D. Cummings

I will praise proper performance every day.

–Paul D. Cummings

I will have the vision of an eagle and the work ethic of a plow horse every day.

–Paul D. Cummings

I will give to others without expectation of return every day.

–Paul D. Cummings

I will be a steward of personal and corporate capital every day.

–Paul D. Cummings

I will operate at Level 10 every day.

–Paul D. Cummings

I will be true to my authentic self every day.

–Paul D. Cummings

I will be a student of those I admire and respect every day.

–Paul D. Cummings

I will be respectful to others every day.

–Paul D. Cummings

I will require our people to follow up with our valued customers every day.

–Paul D. Cummings

I will focus on putting the right player in the right position every day.

–Paul D. Cummings

I will create winning game plans for our team to execute every day.

–Paul D. Cummings

I will demand absolute truth from our team members every day.

–Paul D. Cummings

I will honor all the commitments I make every day.

–Paul D. Cummings

I will be true to my personal convictions every day.

–Paul D. Cummings

I will contribute to the community I live in every day.

–Paul D. Cummings

I will take pride in what we do every day.

–Paul D. Cummings

I will ask high-quality questions every day.

–Paul D. Cummings

I will remember that actions speak louder than words every day.

–Paul D. Cummings

I will operate with a high level of self-discipline every day.

–Paul D. Cummings

I will require our people to come to work with a plan of action every day.

–Paul D. Cummings

I will continue to focus on building and developing talent every day.

–Paul D. Cummings

I will not ever quit. I will keep pushing toward the dream every day.

–Paul D. Cummings

I will be tough and fair in all of my decisions every day.

–Paul D. Cummings

I will use my ability to analyze every day.

–Paul D. Cummings

I will work behind the scenes to improve the organizational climate every day.

–Paul D. Cummings

I will require our people to make dynamic product presentations every day.

–Paul D. Cummings

I will use high-energy music to stimulate our meeting environment every day.

–Paul D. Cummings

I will require our people to do more than they get paid to do every day.

–Paul D. Cummings

I will be dedicated to reaching our organizational goals every day.

–Paul D. Cummings

I will require our people to develop their skills every day.

–Paul D. Cummings

I will manage minutes and moments so my life can be magical every day.

–Paul D. Cummings

I will be rigid in principle but flexible in approach every day.

–Paul D. Cummings

I will remember to focus on my health every day.

–Paul D. Cummings

I will require our people to participate in fun and exciting team-building activities every day.

–Paul D. Cummings

I will be a merchandiser of positive change every day.

–Paul D. Cummings

I will offer guidance to all of our players who need it every day.

–Paul D. Cummings

I will share information with our valued team members every day.

–Paul D. Cummings

I will stay tough through difficult times every day.

–Paul D. Cummings

I will be available to lend a hand when others need me every day.

–Paul D. Cummings

I will remember the value of being a coach every day.

–Paul D. Cummings

I will refuse to show hurt, pain or to quit every day.

–Paul D. Cummings

I will build a mastermind group every day.

–Paul D. Cummings

I will seek out ways to improve our system every day.

–Paul D. Cummings

I will practice what I preach every day.

–Paul D. Cummings

I will enjoy the art of leadership every day.

–Paul D. Cummings

I will be willing to pay a huge price for success every day.

–Paul D. Cummings

I will help destroy any limiting beliefs that might exist every day.

–Paul D. Cummings

I will stand up for those who are right every day.

–Paul D. Cummings

I will require our people to expand their product knowledge every day.

–Paul D. Cummings

I will continue to develop new concepts for our team every day.

–Paul D. Cummings

I will exercise great judgment every day.

–Paul D. Cummings

I will make decisions quickly every day.

–Paul D. Cummings

I will continue to use my creative capacity every day.

–Paul D. Cummings

I will develop clearly defined roles and responsibilities for each player every day.

–Paul D. Cummings

I will constantly strive to improve my leadership techniques every day.

–Paul D. Cummings

I will operate with an uncommon zest every day.

–Paul D. Cummings

I will be willing to invest time in others so they can grow every day.

–Paul D. Cummings

I will require our people to develop winning habits every day.

–Paul D. Cummings

I will think big in all of my planning every day.

–Paul D. Cummings

I will surround myself with strong people every day.

–Paul D. Cummings

I will provide our people with the resources they need to win every day.

–Paul D. Cummings

I will operate with self-awareness every day.

–Paul D. Cummings

I will continue to develop my personal strengths every day.

–Paul D. Cummings

I will listen to others' opinions with an open mind every day.

–Paul D. Cummings

I will be a positive center of influence for our team members every day.

–Paul D. Cummings

I will refuse to panic in the face of adversity every day.

–Paul D. Cummings

I will take adversity and turn it into challenge every day.

–Paul D. Cummings

I will provide every player with individual consideration every day.

–Paul D. Cummings

I will recognize and celebrate the youth in our company every day.

–Paul D. Cummings

I will be a charismatic leader for our people every day.

–Paul D. Cummings

I will require our people to contribute ideas and relevant expertise every day.

–Paul D. Cummings

I will be willing to take calculated risks every day.

–Paul D. Cummings

I will require our people to practice, drill and rehearse every day.

–Paul D. Cummings

I will work to build real trust among team members every day.

–Paul D. Cummings

I will require our people to have maximum fun every day.

–Paul D. Cummings

I will remain objective about myself every day.

–Paul D. Cummings

I will develop a personal code of conduct and stick to it every day.

–Paul D. Cummings

I will be willing to let go of old methodology in order to try new ideas every day.

–Paul D. Cummings

I will break down barriers in our company every day.

–Paul D. Cummings

I will slow down so I can speed up every day.

–Paul D. Cummings

I will do less so I can have more impact every day.

–Paul D. Cummings

I will operate with real balance every day.

–Paul D. Cummings

I will remember the power of dynamic stories every day.

–Paul D. Cummings

I will learn to enjoy the frustrating moments every day.

–Paul D. Cummings

I will be excited about finding solutions for corporate issues every day.

–Paul D. Cummings

I will be up when others are down every day.

–Paul D. Cummings

I will be persistent about dominating the market place every day.

–Paul D. Cummings

I will operate with maximum courage every day.

–Paul D. Cummings

I will remember to stay focused on recruiting new talent every day.

–Paul D. Cummings

I will recognize that my way is not always the right way every day.

–Paul D. Cummings

I will stay on a straight track in my personal and business life every day.

–Paul D. Cummings

I will refuse to "waiver" on the things I believe in every day.

–Paul D. Cummings

I will thank those who point out our mistakes every day.

–Paul D. Cummings

I will be prepared to jump through hoops to make our internal and external customers feel valued every day.

–Paul D. Cummings

I will remember that every person I meet has a flashing sign on his chest that says, "MAKE ME FEEL SPECIAL" every day.

–Paul D. Cummings

I will choose not to operate as a victim every day.

–Paul D. Cummings

I will exercise my power to make great choices every day.

–Paul D. Cummings

I will continue to focus on expanding my intellectual capacity every day.

–Paul D. Cummings

I will be an active participant in a great event every day.

–Paul D. Cummings

I will remember life is either a daring adventure or nothing at all every day.

–Paul D. Cummings

I will make a list of everything I have to be thankful for and review that list every day.

–Paul D. Cummings

I will require our people to build great customer relationships every day.

–Paul D. Cummings

I will exercise and eat right so I can develop more energy every day.

–Paul D. Cummings

I will remember people are the most valuable asset of any organization every day.

–Paul D. Cummings

I will pay close attention to those who are wiser than me every day.

–Paul D. Cummings

I will keep things simple every day.

–Paul D. Cummings

I will sell the benefits of what we do for others every day.

–Paul D. Cummings

I will get up when I fail every day.

–Paul D. Cummings

I will remember there is no shame in losing, only in getting beat every day.

–Paul D. Cummings

I will stay focused on setting new performance records every day.

–Paul D. Cummings

I will remember if my life is worth living, it is worth recording every day.

–Paul D. Cummings

I will learn lessons from the mistakes I make every day.

–Paul D. Cummings

I will pay attention to the fundamental details of my business every day.

–Paul D. Cummings

I will realize I have the ability to make a huge difference every day.

–Paul D. Cummings

I will remember that work is the foundation of all business, the source of all prosperity and the parent of all genius every day.

–Paul D. Cummings

I will recognize the value of my bench players as it applies to reaching the corporate objective every day.

–Paul D. Cummings

I will remember it is healthy to be competitively angry every day.

–Paul D. Cummings

I will learn to say no to the wrong things every day.

–Paul D. Cummings

I will have well-thought agendas published for business meetings every day.

–Paul D. Cummings

I will remember I am one great question away from everything I want in life every day.

–Paul D. Cummings

I will remember the quality of my life is in direct proportion to the quality of the questions I ask or do not ask every day.

–Paul D. Cummings

I will always focus on learning something new every day.

–Paul D. Cummings

I will give my people the authority they need to act every day.

–Paul D. Cummings

I will be a master of conflict resolution every day.

–Paul D. Cummings

I will continue to operate with optimism every day.

–Paul D. Cummings

I will turn our customers into raving fans every day.

–Paul D. Cummings

I will learn that you must sometimes say, "I am wrong" to be a great leader every day.

–Paul D. Cummings

I will always do things to foster teamwork every day.

–Paul D. Cummings

I will not ask our people to sacrifice their family for the benefit of our company every day.

–Paul D. Cummings

I will act today as if my life depended on my best, because my life does depend on my best every day.

–Paul D. Cummings

I will measure everything, because it all matters every day.

–Paul D. Cummings

I will remember education means to draw from the student every day.

–Paul D. Cummings

I will work on becoming a more effective communicator every day.

–Paul D. Cummings

I will learn to thrive during the most chaotic times every day.

–Paul D. Cummings

I will not beat myself up over past failures, but I will embrace the future every day.

–Paul D. Cummings

I will require our people to come to work mentally prepared to work every day.

–Paul D. Cummings

I will train, train, train and then train some more every day.

–Paul D. Cummings

I will master the political landscape in our company every day.

–Paul D. Cummings

I will not let C players drag our A players down every day.

–Paul D. Cummings

I will operate with tenacity in the market place every day.

–Paul D. Cummings

I will remember we are only as strong as our weakest link every day.

–Paul D. Cummings

I will promote the people who deserve to be promoted every day.

–Paul D. Cummings

I will challenge our people to stretch every day.

–Paul D. Cummings

I will always raise the bar, because I know we can do more every day.

–Paul D. Cummings

I will model the excellence of others who are doing great things in the market place every day.

–Paul D. Cummings

I will remember the past does not equal the future every day.

–Paul D. Cummings

I will make certain we deliver a high-quality product to the customer every day.

–Paul D. Cummings

I will devote myself to improving the quality of what we do every day.

–Paul D. Cummings

I will stay unpredictable so our company is energized and excited every day.

–Paul D. Cummings

I will involve our people in important decisions so they feel valued every day.

–Paul D. Cummings

I will recognize the power of a vivid imagination every day.

–Paul D. Cummings

I will look for ways to improve our efficiency every day.

–Paul D. Cummings

I will keep our team safe from "Lackers" every day.

–Paul D. Cummings

I will master the art of negotiating every day.

–Paul D. Cummings

I will be a master closer every day.

–Paul D. Cummings

I will remember that laughter is medicine for the soul every day.

–Paul D. Cummings

I will operate with a long-range perspective every day.

–Paul D. Cummings

I will learn to laugh off the big screw-ups every day.

–Paul D. Cummings

I will keep my eye on the bottom line and the horizon every day.

–Paul D. Cummings

I will not participate in negative meetings. I will find a positive way forward every day.

–Paul D. Cummings

I will recognize the power of managing diversity every day.

–Paul D. Cummings

I will be a strategic thinker every day.

–Paul D. Cummings

I will remember life does not come with an eraser every day.

–Paul D. Cummings

Teacher, Author and CEO Coach **Paul D. Cummings** resides in the Chattanooga, Tennessee area. He is the owner of Paul D. Cummings World Wide Enterprises, a company that is committed to its mission, "Changing Lives Through Dynamic Instruction." Paul teaches and consults for leading companies across the United States, Canada and Europe. He has five children and two grandchildren and is truly of the opinion that "Life is a gift... not a game" (from *Lessons At The Fence Post*).

Paul D. Cummings World Wide Enterprises
1860 Pope Creek Road
Wildwood, Georgia 30757

706-820-9728 • 800-823-7698
info@paulcummings.com • www.paulcummings.com

~ Other Books by Paul D. Cummings ~

- Lessons At The Fence Post
- Lessons At The Fence Post - II

~ Future Titles by Paul D. Cummings ~

- Life Doesn't Come With An Eraser
- The Road To The Top Goes Straight Through The Dump